AFGHANISTAN

PARVAN

BAMIAN

SHEKARI

SHAHIDAN

HINDU KUSH

PANJSHIR

CHAHAR DE-YE
GHOWRBAND

CHARIKAR

BAND-E-AMIR

NIL KOWTAL PASS

SHEBAR
PASS
SAR-E-KOWTAL

DO ABI GHOWR BAND

BAMIAN

QAARSHANATH

KOTTI BABA RANGE

QARAH BAGH

VARDAK

KABUL

TURKMENISTAN

TAJIKISTAN

CHINA

IRAN

KABUL

AFGHANISTAN

PAKISTAN

INDIA

KABUL RIVER

KHYBER PASS

PAKISTAN

LELANDAR

LOWGAR

MILES

0   20   40   60

Band-E-Amir

AFGHAN DREAMS

Young Voices of Afghanistan

TONY O'BRIEN AND MIKE SULLIVAN

PHOTOGRAPHS BY TONY O'BRIEN

BLOOMSBURY
CHILDREN'S
BOOKS

Published by Bloomsbury U.S.A. Children's Books
175 Fifth Avenue, New York, New York 10010

Library of Congress Cataloging-in-Publication Data
O'Brien, Tony.
Afghan dreams : young voices of Afghanistan / by Tony O'Brien and Mike Sullivan ; photographs by
Tony O'Brien. — 1st U.S. ed.
p.   cm.
ISBN-13: 978-1-59990-287-6 • ISBN-10: 1-59990-287-7 (hardcover)
ISBN-13: 978-1-59990-321-7 • ISBN-10: 1-59990-321-0 (reinforced)
1. Teenagers—Afghanistan—Biography—Juvenile literature. 2. Teenagers—Afghanistan—Pictorial
works—Juvenile literature. 3. Children—Afghanistan—Biography—Juvenile literature.
4. Children—Afghanistan—Pictorial works—Juvenile literature. I. Sullivan, Mike. II. Title.
HQ799.A24O27 2008   305.235092'2581—dc2   [B]   2008007004

Typeset in Golden Cockerel ITC
Book design by Daniel Roode

First U.S. Edition 2008
Printed in China
(hardcover) 10 9 8 7 6 5 4 3 2 1
(reinforced) 10 9 8 7 6 5 4 3 2 1

All papers used by Bloomsbury U.S.A. are natural, recyclable products
made from wood grown in well-managed forests. The manufacturing processes
conform to the environmental regulations of the country of origin.

Wheat fields, Bamian

To our families:
Petra, Kiera, Brenna, and Liam
Tina, Marisol, Brendan, Fiona, Kieran, and Arianna
for allowing us to chase our dreams

Afghanistan: Through the Eyes of Her Children

Afghanistan is often defined by the borders of its neighbors: northwest of Pakistan and Hindustan (India), east of Iran, south of Russia, west of China. Its valleys have provided trade routes for centuries. Several branches of the great Silk Road ran through the passages they offered. They also dictated the route of countless invasions. Early on, it was Semiramis—who became queen of Babylon after her bravery in the capture of Bactra—then Sargon of Assyria, Cyrus the Great of Persia, and Alexander the Great of Macedon; later, it was Great Britain then Russia, and now the Taliban and the United States.

We had come to Afghanistan to talk with children. It is a country at war with itself and a country that has been a pawn in the wars of imperial interests for centuries. "The Great Game," as the British called it, continues in this tribal land: foreign powers vying for control of important trade routes and vast mineral deposits, Afghan warlords fighting for money and power. This was Mike's first visit to Afghanistan; as a freelancer and on assignment for *LIFE* magazine, Tony had covered the Afghan insurgency against the Soviets and the years following until the Taliban seized power. When Tony returned in 2004 after the American invasion, he found many Afghans filled with a sense of hope.

Now, as hope fades, who killed a child's parents, brothers, sisters is often an accident of time, place, and the child's age. For the young Afghanis between the ages of eight and fifteen whom we interviewed, the killers were usually the Taliban, and at times the mujahideen (Afghan guerilla fighters). If we had interviewed their older siblings or parents, it would have been the Russians. If we had talked to their grandparents, the British. At one school we saw a UN poster warning the children not to touch mines, bomblets, grenades, or any unexploded ordnance. We were dismayed to see that the markings on the illustration were all from American arms. Fifteen years ago in Afghanistan, the same posters with the same warnings showed Russian markings.

Hillside in Kabul

We asked the children we met about their past, their families, their present lives, and their hopes for the future. Some of the children had definite dreams of what they wanted to happen in their lives; at times these dreams were quite sophisticated. Some children were so burdened by the daily struggle that they seldom looked beyond the moment. The differences were random, independent of ethnic group or social status; optimism and pessimism lived arm in arm. Dreamers and realists shared school lessons in the mornings and work in the afternoons.

Often we told the children the story of Aladdin and his magic lamp and asked what their three wishes would be. At times we sensed that the answers were influenced by the fact that they were addressing outsiders, foreigners. But the overwhelming desire for education was genuine. Children who had been denied school for so many years had a burning desire for education and peace. Mukhtar, our translator, explained that education is truly their dream, although for many it is out of their reach. Their reality is this poverty-stricken, war-torn country.

In countless war-ravaged countries around the globe, people are carrying on with the basic necessities of survival. Occasionally, there is something more, a sign of hope. In Kabul there is a wide boulevard. On one side is the damaged university; on the other side is a neighborhood reduced to rubble. At the terminus of the boulevard is the bombed-out shell of a government palace. Nothing grows. We were told that before the recent wars there were tall trees on both sides, and the avenue was covered with a carpet of leaves in the fall. Sometime after the battles between the mujahideen groups destroyed this part of the city, someone planted saplings along the boulevard. They seem a fitting metaphor of hope—the saplings and the children of Afghanistan.

—Tony O'Brien & Mike Sullivan, Santa Fe, 2008

Boys carrying bread, Kabul

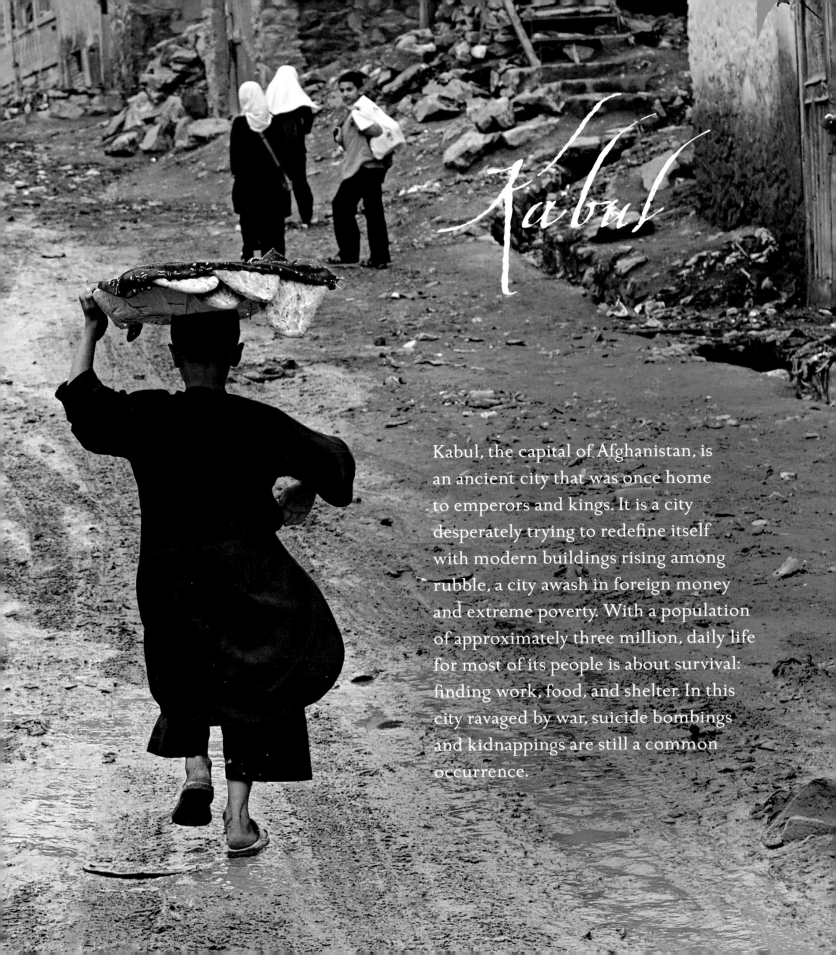

Kabul

Kabul, the capital of Afghanistan, is an ancient city that was once home to emperors and kings. It is a city desperately trying to redefine itself with modern buildings rising among rubble, a city awash in foreign money and extreme poverty. With a population of approximately three million, daily life for most of its people is about survival: finding work, food, and shelter. In this city ravaged by war, suicide bombings and kidnappings are still a common occurrence.

Nozoku

Age: 10

Kabul, Aschiana Literacy Program

I buy spand [incense] from a shop close to my school. I put it in a small can that I give to my sisters, and they sell it in the bazaar to the espandi boys. In a day we make twenty or thirty afghani [forty to sixty cents].

What makes me sad is war and suicide attacks. I heard the explosion the other day. I was here at school. A while ago there were American troops passing close to the bus I was on. Then a motorcycle passed with a suicide bomb. There were some poor people near the attack and they were killed. I get sick and nervous worrying about the attacks. I hope it ends.

I am happy when I learn a lot. I would be happy if someday I know enough to be a teacher.

Nasir

Age: 14
Kabul

I work as an espandi. If you are my customer, I espand (incense) your car or your shop. It brings you good luck, and your work will go well. Because I espand the others they have good luck, but in my life I don't have luck. If I stop work to go to school, my stepmother will be angry. So for my future it is not clear what will happen.

Asmat

Age: 13
Kabul

I used to be in school, but I didn't understand the lessons, and I failed the test. I would like to study, to go back to school, but there is no chance. If a child from another country came here I would show him my life, what I do each day, and that for my future I have nothing.

The other espandi (Nasir, left) is my best friend. We start work early in the morning and espand until two in the afternoon. At two I go home, wash my hands, and pray.

Rohul Ali

Age: 14
Kabul, bakery

During the Taliban time we went to Iran; there was no work or schools in Afghanistan. There I went to school until fifth grade. Then I quit to go to work, first as a mechanic and painting cars, then in a bakery.

We returned to our home and now my cousin rents this bakery. Four of my brothers work here. Someday I would like us to have our own shop. Then I could get married.

If I met children from another country I would ask what they study in school, and what they want for the future. Children in America have the same ideas as me, because we are children, we are as brothers.

Ayisha Hasea Qadir

Age: 14

Kabul, Freedom Afghanistan Girls' School

I want to be a journalist and travel all over, to America, Australia, and India, as well as Afghanistan. I want to talk to the sick people, the poor people, and bring their words back here to put on the news. If there is a need for me to have a family I will marry, but if there is no need, then I won't. When I am a journalist I will take care of myself. I will marry my profession.

Jalalideen

Age: 18 (boy in red shirt)
Kabul, in the family's rug-weaving shop and home
(the three at right are siblings)

I was in Afghanistan during the wars. We couldn't get out. For a time we stayed in Parvan province. I was lucky that no one in my immediate family died, but some of my relatives were killed.

I am eighteen, in my last year of school. I work making carpets from early morning until one, then I go to school.

I would like to build houses, something people can use, not big buildings. When I am twenty-five I will start looking for a wife, but even fifty is not too old to get married.

Mohammed Ashraf

Age: 16 (above, striped shirt)

I work in the morning making carpets; in the afternoon I go to school.

I would like to be a doctor, the kind who makes artificial legs. No one in my family has need of one; I would do it just because I like it.

Faridah

Age: 16 (above center, right)

I also work in the morning making carpets, and then I go to school. I work hard and am ranked third in my class. We have studied Germany. I'd like to go there. I want to discover new things, to know what no one else does. Then I could teach; I'd like to teach third grade.

I am accustomed to wartime; that's all I know.

Majaasin

Age: 11

Kabul, Afghanistan National Association for the Deaf

I am the youngest in my family. I go to school here with my two older sisters. My life at home is good. I live with my family. We own our house. At school I learn about things we need for life. With education we have a chance to get a job in the future.

In this artwork (below), the circles represent villages, cities, and small camps where the Kuchi nomads live. They are usually in isolated places in the desert or by the mountains, far from cities. The big circle is Kabul; if you see it from the mountains, it covers a big area. There is a woman with children, a baba (an old man), and some sheep.

The large painting (see pages 20–21) shows war, the jirga, and peacetime. Two classmates and myself made this painting. It shows the Taliban time, the killing, the hard times, then the fight between the Taliban and the mujahideen. In the center is the jirga, the leaders of Afghanistan coming together, discussing how to rebuild the country. And to the left is Afghanistan at peace. It shows Afghanistan rebuilt. I am a part of that, I am there, but I am not represented directly.

When I finish twelfth grade I hope to go to university and be a teacher, or possibly a manager in this center. But my dream is painting. I like painting birds, gardens, beautiful places. If children came from another country I would show them my pictures, everything I've drawn, everything I've done with my hands.

Fatanah

Age: 10
Kabul, Afghanistan National
Association for the Deaf

At home I help my mother and I can talk by signing with my uncle. He helps us. I would like a big garden, with a thousand trees and lots of different fruits. We are poor—my mother does laundry. So I would ask Aladdin for money for clothes, notebooks, and pens. And I would like a house.

If I could fly I would fly myself to Holland, because it has good weather. I want to see the gardens, the green places, and the red flowers. I don't want to cut the flowers, just see them from up close.

Said Hakim

Age: 14
Kabul, tailor shop

At the Kabul zoo, I've seen the lion, the monkeys, and the pigeons. I like drawing them when I'm at school.

When I grow up I hope to be a mechanic and to marry. I don't have anyone in mind, but I really like my aunt Sam's daughter. She is thirteen. I don't know if she likes me.

From Aladdin I would like a good house, a car, and that girl I like.

My father and three of my brothers died. The Taliban came to Bamian and killed them. I was so small, I don't remember their being killed, but I remember when the neighbor carried my father into the house. After my father died, I told my mother to take my brother and me and go to Kabul, because my uncle was bothering us. We had a donkey and a cow in Bamian. But my uncle wanted them for himself. Because of that we left Bamian.

Wahaab

Age: 10

Kabul, marketplace

I have been working as a thief for twenty days, stealing from people's pockets. I've done it ten times, it's true, ten times in twenty days.

I want my real father to come back, I want my sisters and brothers, and I want a house.

Shaheen

Age: 10

Kabul, police station

There are six people in my family. My father died six years ago.

I was selling plastic boxes in the bazaar. A boy named Jumadeen came and said, "Work with me and you will make 1,000 or 1,500 afghani a day." He said, "Come and watch me. I will pick a pocket and you will see how much I earn in a second." He went and robbed someone, and got 700 afghani. I saw it was a way to make money very easily, so I started this work. Nazeer came to me and said, "If you steal for me and the police take you to the station, I will come and get you out." I started being a pickpocket with my friend twenty days ago. I've done it five times.

[What do you think will happen to you now?]
   Jail.

Nasi

Age: 13

Kabul, Aschiana Literacy Program

I work in the bazaar all morning selling plastic boxes, then in the afternoons I am here in the Aschiana center. I study music, math, Dari [a variation of the Persian language], the Koran, and sports. I like to sing the taranaas. They are a type of folk song.

When I grow up I want to be a singer and a teacher. There are children working in the bazaar who have no good future. I want to teach them, to give them hope.

Gul Mohammed

Age: 12

Kabul, Muratani neighborhood

We stayed in this neighborhood during the fighting between the Taliban and the mujahideen. During the Taliban time there was no school, but now I am studying Dari, English, Pashtu, science, math, sports, and the holy book.

I sell peppers from a karachi [wheeled cart] from eight until ten in the mornings. Then I go to public school from noon to four in the afternoon, then sell peppers again until seven. The peppers are fresh; one kind is sweet, the other is dry and salty. In one day I can make from 200 to 500 afghani [four to ten dollars].

I can never stay in one place; the police make me move. Sometimes they beat me or break the tires of my cart, and won't let me stay and sell the peppers. After they beat us they might take the karachi to the police station. In the evening if you pay 100 afghani they will let it go. If you can't pay, they keep the karachi for a week. They usually ask for 50 or 100 afghani, depending on the size of the cart. I don't know why they do this. Lately they haven't been taking the carts, just beating us. I have never been hurt too badly, but sometimes they beat us with wood, or they throw away the peppers. I never give the police money.

Zahaib

Age: 15
Kabul

I have made some friends here, but the schools are not good. Teachers say the pay is low, and they can't use their energy teaching us. My friends say go to courses outside—you can't learn in public school. Teachers tell us to go home and find the answer; they don't teach. All the kids say study English to get a job with an NGO [non-government organization].

I don't want to "date." The cops put you in jail for two or three days if you try. If you walk by a girls' school and tell someone, "You are pretty," undercover cops come. You can only talk to the opposite sex in class, not in the street.

Jeena

(sister to Zahaib, left)
Age: 16
Kabul

My mother is broad-minded; most families marry off their daughters at fifteen or sixteen or seventeen years old. It is hard for girls here. If they work outside people say bad things. They say it is not good for a woman to go out; they should stay at home and be a housewife. Many girls say, "At fifteen or eighteen we are going to be married. We don't need an education." But most girls do want an education.

My friends want to study English and computers. The teachers at school just give lectures, then go home. I go to an outside class for computers at six in the morning, before school, but my family won't let me go to outside classes that are coed. I can't go against the wishes of my family.

I would like to go outside Afghanistan to university, then return to help make my country independent of outside help.

Abdul Jalil

Age: 15

Kabul, Window of Hope Orphanage

I was born in Paktia. When I was three years old I was sick and my uncle took me to a doctor. While we were gone the mujahideen shot a rocket into my house, and everyone was killed. I stayed at my uncle's farm for eight years, then came to Kabul. I am happy here. I have become accustomed to the other children at the orphanage.

The Paktia people have a very special respect for guests. My favorite place there is called Balley Sar; it means "a high place." I was happy there. It was not destroyed in the war.

Farima

Age: 13
Kabul, Freedom Afghanistan Girls' School

When the war started we went to Pakistan. It was hard. We had to pay rent for the house, but had little money. We couldn't go to school. We went there in 1382 and came back in 1385. [To convert the Iranian calendar to a western year, add 621.]

For children from another country I would make mentu. It is like dill balls with meat inside. Usually we put yogurt and garlic on top. And also I would make buloni, dill filled with spinach and meat, or potatoes and meat.

The most important things in my life are my mother and father. I love them very much. The most important thing that can happen in my country is peace—to live peacefully and be able to continue my studies.

Boys in a cemetery flying a kite over Kabul

Ihsan

Age: 13

Kabul, kite maker's shop

There are thirteen people in my family, five brothers, six sisters, and my parents. Two of my sisters are married. Now they are working in the other room making kites. I have been making kites for six years. I make good kites, different sizes, different designs. I make the design myself and cut out the paper. I put symbols for peace on my kites. It is hard to cut the bamboo. We cut it very thin. If it is not made just right it won't fly. The paper comes from Germany, from Pakistan, and from Iran. The glue is from Kabul.

When I make the kites, it makes children happy. Everyone is happy because of kites. We export kites from here to different cities. Pakistan and Mazar-e Sherif. I've seen the kites from those places, but the best ones are from Kabul.

The kites my older sister makes are very beautiful. My sisters and mother make kites but they don't fly them. That is work for boys.

Parwiz

Age: 12

Kabul, Afghanistan National Association for the Deaf

I cannot hear or speak, and in my house there are two others the same way, both of them girls.

I like all subjects in school. We learn about everything, but my favorite is religion and the Dumiat [the study of correct living according to Islam]. Some of the teachers here teach by signing, others use writing and reading.

Every day that there is time I go to the mosque, and the mullah preaches. I can only watch him and see that he is speaking; there is no one to translate. I would go more often if there was someone to sign.

In my family only my mother knows any signing, but she is not proficient. Aside from her there is no one to sign with me.

Nadira

Age: 11

Kabul, carpet maker's home

*I have been working on the carpets for six years.
Because of the work I don't go to school. I would like
to go; my family would like me to be in school.*

*There are eight in the family, and four make the
rugs. I don't know how much I make in a day; the
money goes to the family. I start at five in the morning
and finish at seven at night.*

Mohammed Rabi

Age: 12
Kabul

I like soccer. I want to be a goalkeeper. In the future I am sure I will be tall. I want to play on the Afghan team and go to other countries to play. I would ask players from other places about good techniques for playing, for tips on how to be a good player.

If they came here, I would show them the special Afghani tricks that they don't know. There are special things we do here. After the game I would show them the old historic sites in Kabul and exhibitions in museums. It is important for friends to know about that.

Rhamat

Age: 11

Kabul, food shop

I am eleven years old and in fourth grade. I go to school from ten in the morning until one. Then I work in my father's tailor shop or his food shop. When I finish school I would like to be a mechanic fixing cars and motorcycles.

I would like to show children from another country my shop, the bazaar, and the zoo. My favorite animals are the monkeys and a small cow. It would be nice to work at the zoo. I would feed the animals. I would especially like to take care of the cow.

Fardin

Age: 12

Kabul, Aschiana School

I used to work collecting paper and cartons from different places for burning. After that I was washing cars with two of my brothers. We take all the money and give it to my mother, and she buys the bread and rice for home.

Here at Aschiana I am in the painting class. I would like to paint buzkashi. A buzkash man rides a horse; in the game everyone has horses. There is a circle, and in the circle there is a dead goat. The rider picks up the goat and tries to take it to his goal and throw it there. The other side tries to stop him and take the goat to their goal.

Neelab

Age: 14

Kabul, Afghans4Tomorrow School #1

My parents always tell me to study, to go to school and learn something. In the future I want to be a judge. People come to a judge if one person is having problems with another, if someone takes somebody else's rights. The judge solves the problem and makes people happy and friendly again.

I think a young person can be a judge—a twenty-year-old can be one.

Tajalaa

Age: 8
Kabul, Aschiana

I live on the peak of a mountain with my mother and one small brother. There is no electricity. We live with a lamp and carry our water up on our backs. We have lived up there for five or six years.

I remember my father. He was a very kind man. He brought us food and clothes. He always said for us to go to school, but unfortunately my mother says now we have to work. At home we drink chai [tea] and eat naan [bread].

When I grow up I would like to have a family of five or six sons. I only want boys. The most important thing I could give them is milk and bread.

The mountains of Bamian

The Countryside

Afghanistan is a hard and dazzling country divided by the snow-capped mountains of the Hindu Kush. Leaving the cities, one steps back in time. Most of the country lacks electricity and running water, and transportation is mainly by foot. Many of the villages are almost the same as they were hundreds of years ago, and the people, like the country, are beautiful and dignified, with a wildness to them. Hospitality is an ancient tradition that is cherished and lavished on visitors of all kinds.

Jan Bibi

Age: 10
Lelandar

I am from Asman Qala (asman means "sky" and qala means "big house with a wall").
I have three brothers, three sisters. One brother fell from a tree while cutting leaves
for the goats. He was killed. After school I work with my mother collecting blackberries
from the fields and drying them. They are for eating during the winter.

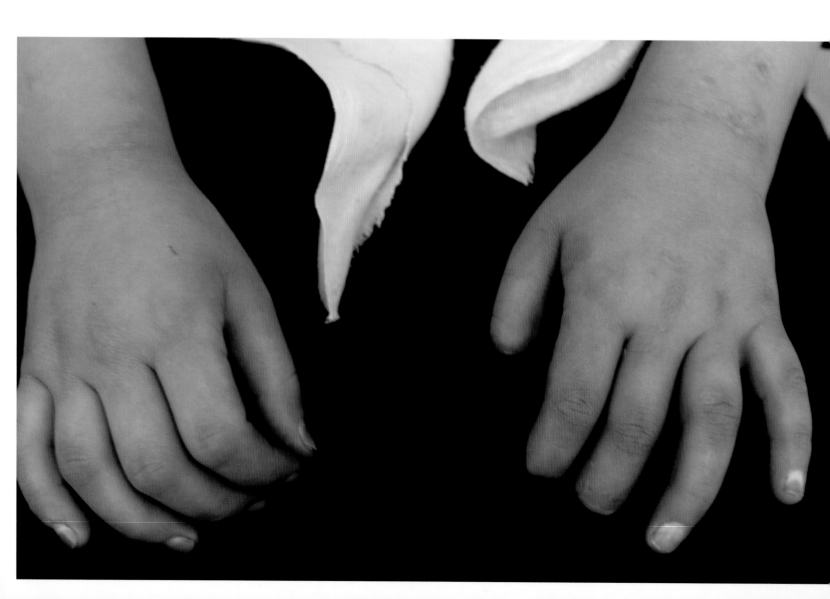

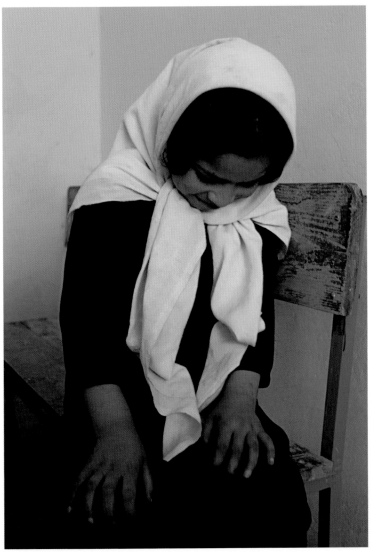

The teachers have warned us about the mines from the Russian war. Twice my father has exploded mines, but he is alive. He was working in the mountains. He stepped on a mine. His foot is damaged, and he has something in his chest.

Six months ago I found the pistol that hurt my hand and my face. I hit it with a rock and it blew off my fingers.

When I hurt my hand there was no doctor here, no car, not even bandages. So they took me to Kabul in a truck.

Bilquis

Age: 15
Shahidan, Village School

During the violence we moved to Saighan, about fifteen hours' walk from here. We stayed there six months. My father, uncle, and grandfather were killed.

I would take visiting children to my family: show them my house and the historical places, Band-e Amir, the Buddha, and what we grow in our fields. We would give them yogurt and buttermilk.

We try to learn in order to develop our country. What we learn here we will teach others. I would like to become a teacher, and if the government accepts me, teach here in Shahidan. But it is not my decision. I hope it will happen.

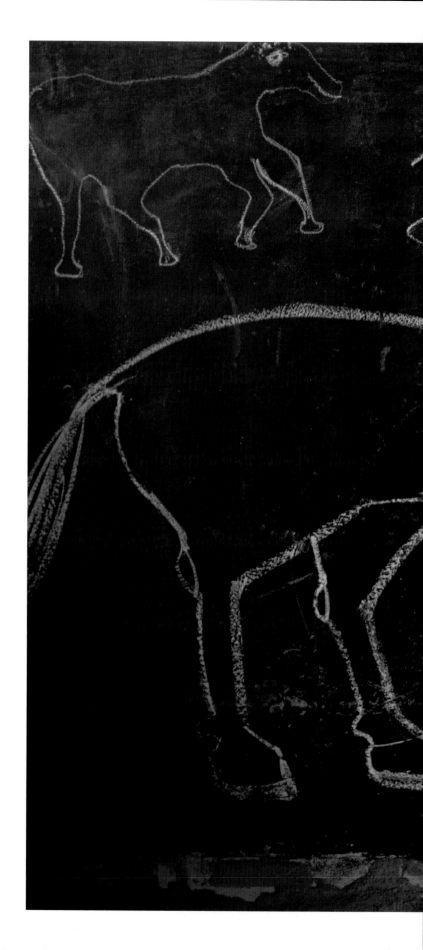

Kamila

(far left)
Age: 14
Bamian

We walk two hours each way to school. We are very tired afterward, and it is hard to do our studies.

I want to be a midwife. It is very necessary; many women die in childbirth. For my own children I want education most of all.

During the Taliban we mostly lived in the mountains in Panjsher. I was very sad when they blew up the Buddha statue.

Barrat Khan

Age: 13
Chahar dehe Ghurband

In the restaurant upstairs I work as a waiter.

I want to be a teacher. I would like to show visiting children the gardens of the village. I'd ask them, How are the schools in your country? What is your society like? I would ask them to help us get an education. For Afghanistan I hope for peace, and that the people will become prosperous.

Zahara

Age: 13

Bamian

A person who doesn't know English is not educated. I want to visit Hindustan [India] and America. I have seen movies from India on TV, but I do not want to be an actress.

For Afghanistan I want peace and development. I would show visiting children the Buddha statues and the Taliban gun emplacements on the mountain. I would ask them if they have sculptures like we do here, and if they have fields like ours.

Ismaat

Age: 13

Qarghanatu, teahouse

I have never been to school. I am too old now. I would have liked to go to school. I wouldn't want to go anywhere, just to stay here.

All the village had to move during the Taliban time. We went to a village called Bessud, one day walking. There is no road. Our village was destroyed. Through the winter we fought with them. They came back in the summer and took all the animals. About five hundred people died in this valley, mostly of starvation.

Bibi Aisha

Age: 11

Sutir Faridah, Lelandar

I have never been out of Lelandar; during the fighting I was here in the village of Sutir Faridah [flying camel]. My oldest brother was killed in the Russian war. That was before I was born.

We are four sisters. Three come to school. One is older than fifteen and my parents don't let her come to school. Often there is not enough food in the house and the older people have to work hard.

I would love to believe in a magic carpet—I would use it to fly home from school. It takes me one hour to walk; I could fly there in five minutes. But I wouldn't want to go on a flying camel. We don't have one of those. It is an old name, Sutir Faridah. Maybe there were flying camels then.

Najmudin

Age: 13
Bamian

I hope to be a teacher, to bring the light to other children. I want to be a teacher of teachers.

Acknowledgments:

We wish to offer our humble thanks to the following people and organizations for their help in the making of this book:

Sabrina Omar, Farhad Said, Sayed Mohammed, Shaheen Rassoul, Molly Howitt, Kathy Gannon, DeePak Puri, David Krause, Peter Ellzey, Jerry Courvoisier, Jack Loeffler, David Scheinbaum, Steve Dunn, Jeanne Arnold, and Pamela Burnham.

Afghanistan National Association for the Deaf—Abdul Gaffar; Turquoise Mountain Foundation—Rameen Moshref Javid; Aschiana—Nazar Mohammad; Afghans4Tomorrow—Soraya Omar; Future Generation—Homyra Itimadi; Window of Hope-House of Children—Mohammed Sabir; Hope Worldwide Afghanistan—Kelli Reinhardt; Central Asia Institute—Greg Mortenson; Canon USA—Amy Kawadler.

There are those who deserve a few words and whom we would like to offer a deep bow: our translator, driver, fellow dreamer, and friend, Mukhtar Shah; Wakil Shakir of the Central Asia Institute for moments not forgotten; the Jerga; and the newly built Lelandar school. Special thanks to the children who touched us on our journey, and to Victoria Wells Arms, our editor, for her belief in the book and in us and most of all for her belief in the children and letting their words have a voice.

Thank you and all who supported us along our way. —T. O. & M. S.

And especially thanks to Nadr Ali, my friend, my soul mate, my brother; you are with me always, until the next time, Inshallah.

I learned in Afghanistan the most cherished thing in life for me is family, my tribe. How can I thank mine, past and present: perhaps with a book of dreams? Thank you for believing. —T. O.

Afghanistan School for the Deaf, Kabul

Malalie School, Char Asiab (village)

DATE DUE

OC 25 97			
AR 30 '98			
NV 13 '98			
DE 18 '98			
AP 6 99			

DEMCO 38-296

HUBBLE